CHILD BALLAD

DAVID WHEATLEY

CHILD BALLAD
DAVID WHEATLEY

WAKE FOREST UNIVERSITY PRESS

First North American edition.
Published in Ireland and the UK
by Carcanet Press in 2023.

For permission, write to
Wake Forest University Press
Post Office Box 7333
Winston-Salem, NC 27109
WFUPRESS.WFU.EDU

ISBN 978-1-943667-11-6 (paperback)
LCCN 2023945272

Designed and typeset by
Nathan Moehlmann, Goosepen Studio & Press.

Printed and bound in Canada by Friesens.

Cover illustration: Attributed to William Mosman,
*Sir James Macdonald 1741–1766 and Sir Alexander
Macdonald 1744/1745–1795*. National Galleries
of Scotland. Purchased 1967.

Publication of this book was made possible
by generous support from the Boyle Family Fund.

CONTENTS

11 The Companions of Colmcille

12 Bucksburn

13 Stay

15 Go Down Easy

17 Brush

18 Composition with Farmyard Animals

19 To a Damselfly

20 Helen Mabel Trevor, *The Fisherman's Mother*

21 To Nan Shepherd in the Cairngorms

23 Old Nuns' Graves

24 Adomnán's Sermon to the Oil Rigs

25 A Lecture on the Newton Stone

27 A Diurnal Upon St. Lucy's Day

29 Mr. Green

30 Child Ballad

32 Homage to Inverurie

34 A Compressed Aggregate

36 "You found me like a pebble"

37 Northborough Sonnets

41 Dyspraxia Ode

43 Ellis O'Connor, *West No. 3*

44 Landscape with Heavy Industry and Washing Line

46 Aberdeen Elegy

47 One Door May Conceal Another

48 Dear Cliff Forshaw

50 Portrait of a Man Thought to Be Andrew Marvell

52 In Search of the Tenderer Thorns

53 In Stranraer

55 To Lough Tay

57 Flags and Emblems

59 Mouth Music

60 Our Lady of the Snows

62 Child Ballad

63 The Bothy at Tillyfourie
64 Wolf-Girl, Clais Mhadaidh
66 The Fourth Craw
69 Poem beginning with line spoken by a toddler
70 Paysage moralisé
71 Immigrant Song
73 Granite Elegy/Dàn do Eibhir
75 A Pine Wood in North Africa
77 A Sconser Tartan
79 Reliquary
80 Souterrain
81 A Clashindarroch Wildcat for Tom Pickard
84 Stanzas for a Lover
85 To the River Don
87 Gaelic Lane Elegy
89 Alteration
90 Three Ponies
92 Chiaroscuro
93 Long Slide
94 Two from Reverdy
96 The Enigma of Arrival
97 Glow
98 Line-Breaks
99 Marriage
100 A Return
101 Un/Settled
102 Зеркала
105 A Curious Herbal

133 Acknowledgments

for Felix and Morven

CHILD BALLAD

DAVID WHEATLEY

The Companions of Colmcille

If I never go home it is because
the tides, I have noticed, flow in one direction
only. With Viking anger the North Sea
snapped at my heels on the foreshore as I
marveled at its circling, patterned collapse,
the golden spiral in my Euclid turning
before my eyes. When the Covenanter
who led me arrived at the city gates
he would not pay the king's penny
to cross the bridge but stood transfixed
by those swithering waters. The road was closed,
he told me, we would have to go back.
I saw the long-beaked oystercatchers gazing
down from their nests along the flat roofs
and knew this for the place where Devenick,
Ternan and Drostan had passed before me, drawn
ever further north and east. I swore an oath
at the mercat cross to a man who answered
to the Earl of Montrose, and a prayer-book
was placed in my hand. Much later, when
the peace was won, bodies decently buried
were exhumed and despoiled, marking
an end to it all. I attempted to read the psalms
in the vernacular, but did not know
what language that was. If you throw out a hand
in the dark of the chapel a door to the bell-tower
will be there, and a view from above that promised
once, not now, to make everything clear.

1644

Bucksburn

Or: the hired box down a lane. You
could walk to the airport for coffee
or wait for the new conference center
that duly, out of nowhere, arrived—
that or the pub on the hill lit
like an abattoir. I'd come back from work
to find you in the ruined cottage next door
stepping out of/into the pages of *Sunset Song*,
the Scots words seeding on your tongue
with every turn of the harrow in
the neighboring field. The deer
came to our window and the siskins
came through the cat flap—bite-sized
portions of wilderness here at the city's edge.
Of an evening we sat on alphabetized
book boxes, our steerage fellow travelers,
never unpacked as long as we stayed.
To use the phone you had to stand on a table
in the corner, reaching absurdly upwards.
Children, here we first knocked
on your door, with no reply. The grass
grew over our ankles and we fled
to the country in time for the summer, west
and north where the mountains have girls' names,
where the harvest comes late and heavy.

Stay

1

Baby of mine descending
from the nurse's arms
into your mother's like
a heron approaching its nest

2

and unpacking its legs
baby born to a creeping
autumn hungry for dark
you kick your heels in the gap

3

of light where dawn and dusk
rub backs in the trough
of winter and son of mine
silently mouth your name

4

with fluttering tongue
after so long in the pulsing
tunnel all walls
are theatre curtains parting

5

between one breast and the next
you defy with a fallen-
limp fist the single
bedroom that is the world

6

and here is the tree whose shadow
passing over the bed
will trace like a blind man's
hand your features and here

7

a single tear of milk
lining your cheek until
when I look away it is
only to reenter

8

the moment from the echoing
shell of its promise and will
it stay now you child are
the lamp and you are the genie

Go Down Easy

Too long I
waited for
the name of
the flower
I did not
know to show
itself at first
light & now
though nights
are days &
days are nights
I wake to us
a room with
you in it
companionable
form our spoon-
faced dollop
served up hot
I feel our
breath re-
circulate from
mouth to mouth
as the morning
digger in the
back field paws
at the moon
but the moon is
yours and the
mirror laughs
before you do
so let me sing
the things you bring

your mother's
face swum
into the light
while a frisky
ghost cat's
tail brushes
your middle
name & your
pointed finger
points at itself

Brush

Assisted
first steps on
the mountain

feet brushing it
sideways like smooth
jazz drumming

carry you never-
theless to
the threshold of

our grip
beyond which for
the moment

there is nothing
you understand
nothing

Composition with Farmyard Animals

Are you my avatar	left and right
I mentally steer you	through the farmyard
raising a dust-cloud	from hens on the path
as I amble behind	and you my small

smudge in the sun	are my point
of focalization	asleep beneath a square
of billowing red	where the light of morning
breathes color	the sun brims over

the daylight moon	is small change
and further moon	upon moon rises
in your mother's nails	round her coffee mug
use of the imperative	tense affirms

the principle of	selection in the visual field
let today's sky be	mauve or cerise
and over the breakfast	table find a painting
Oranges et ananas	of the food on your plate

we shall stroll	among farm buildings
and follow the hens	through the library
from Ten Little Pirates	ours we learn
is a world with	subtraction in it

and unexpected	restoration of all
that was lost	the hen blinks
we vanish and reappear	that's not a way
that's a way	to the pond and here

we learn too	awaiting the paused
angle of her next	step to drop
is the hopscotch path	we will take
to a world of	tentative absolutes

To a Damselfly

Your wing is a chambered eye,
your glassy wing that prints its
airy view on the freeze-framed
flight paths that you trail flying
by. Cryptic-colored female,
you come in to land over
the cow parsley on legs that
cannot walk but only stand.
The sweating, late-July sky's
a porous edge of havoc;
fanning your stigma markings
wide you relaunch into your
element, a pond of heat
and color dragged for prey. The
pulse of summer keeps time with
your inaudible hum, and
you are the line all day long
between trees, water and sky,
the world's loose stitch and its thread.

Helen Mabel Trevor, The Fisherman's Mother

for Ailbhe Darcy

Saint Anne has appeared to a ploughman;
Saint Anne is the fisherman's mother,
who sowed Christ's swaddling clothes and his shroud.
The pilgrim's name is Misery, her
face worn like a stone by the flood. The
coiffe, the lace headscarf, can also be
worn under a hood. Should you require
it she is all Irish womanhood:
my whole life long I have sat in the
parlor under her accipitrine
gaze. She is the artist in age; burns
leaves by a pond amid memories
of Frank O'Meara, malarial,
dead. The pilgrims dragged themselves three times
round the church on their bare knees, no less.
In this interior we are free
of the sound of their prayers, of the goose-
girl and her prattling-trafficked charges.
I drew a watercolor of a
watercolor left out in the rain,
but could not match the solid lines of
the woman's hands on her blackthorn stick
sweating oil paint and years. I too have
dipped my hands in miraculous springs
where pustular Jobs have filled their bowls,
have washed one hand with the other in
the dark not knowing who else is there;
repeat the words of the Rosary
to someone who repeats after me,
not knowing whose voice it is I hear.

To Nan Shepherd in the Cairngorms

You will not be finding
        a thing but in
the place where it will be
        you will not
be losing a thing
        but in the place

where it's not
        spinning the compass
confounding available
        coordinates these
great gashes in
        the field of the sky

and the red over
        grey of the feldspar
corries where saxifrage
        the rock-breaker
lifts white flags
        of resistance

and arctic flowers glow
        from their brush
with the ice-age
        when the boy
died in the snowdrift
        he was found

on his knees as though
        in a posture of
prayer the snow god
        will swallow you
whole and leave
        you untouched

the peak we approach through
       the cloud is not
this peak but the next one
       the mountain
we stand on is not this
       one but the next

Old Nuns' Graves

How to do it   to float above history
at just the right angle   refusing
like these plumes   of gorse fires
all definition   or old nuns' graves
their real names   buried elsewhere

their church keeps   seasonal hours
a part-time Christ   for the part-time redeemed
the path in the woodlands   is circular
we retreat from   the uneven ground
only to come round   again

my faithless epiphanies   had shrunk
in memory   to an unwilling boyhood
convent visit   spent prowling
corridors filled   with my roars
and the lone old   nun receding

down the long   passage that smelt
of disinfectant   past rows
of doors ajar   on empty cells
their secrets nothing   a bleached
vacancy could   not absorb

Adomnán's Sermon to the Oil Rigs

I argued with the Irish over the date of Easter
and saw in a vision hills of fire out at sea.

I have known the holy places—Egypt, Rome,
Jerusalem—from staring out over the waves

where brackish streams tickle my threshold and
I wake to a whelk on my palm and my beard afloat.

I saw the sandstorm coming and built my chapel
on sand. I would number the oil-fields named for saints

and seabirds: *Ninian, Columba, Shearwater,*
Auk. Sea-spray and thunder; kittiwake's egg

of a scarred moon. I sense Ninian's faint candle
out in the North Sea and the gannet scissoring up

to daylight from the depths, his beak full of ship-
wrecked souls. I turn first to bone and legend,

then to bone and legend dispersed into sand.

A Lecture on the Newton Stone

for Jeremy Noel-Tod

A star collapse, unimaginable
dark energies turned in on themselves:
likewise these misplaced civilizations,
the anti-matter of millennia leaving
only fingerprints on standing stones.
I came when the man digging the ditch called out,
stunned by the protuberance.[1] Now
the huge mossed-over phallus swives the sky,
the point-seam of the ogham snaking up
the left-hand side in a hopeless medley
of proper names: "lies here... son of the priest
of... offspring..."[2] Eagle, dolphin, and wolf
are written first on the stone of the skin,
are ranks made manifest, the comb and mirror
that other natural order matriarchy.
Our concern though is the central script,
a tremor felt in someone else's blood,
the names mysterious and a swastika
prominently inserted. It would seem
that Pictish was a sort of Bolshevism
of the tongue, capable of anything.[3]
Forswear the Aryan hypothesis,
nor are you looking at Phoenician.[4] Still,
nothing quite like it had been found before.
The Irish saint addressed the natives through
an interpreter, and this proves *nothing*:
the circles on the symbol stone do *not*
spin only to grind out theories on
the Christian god: they are their own thing
and I mine, crossing the garage forecourt
under the red moon to the Crichie stones
to keep my fierce appointment with the new

1. G. F. Browne, *On Some Antiquities in the Neighbourhood of Dunecht House, Aberdeenshire* (1921), 110–124.

2. W. F. Skene, "Notes on the Ogham Inscription of the Newton Stone," *Proceedings of the Society of Antiquaries of Scotland* (1865), 289–298.

3. Gillechriosd Moraidh Mac a' Ghreidhir, "Irish Lessons for Scottish Nationalists," *Modern Scot* (April 1931).

4. Cf. George Moore, *Ancient Pillar Stones of Scotland* (1865).

and old gods, be they present or no.
What they want, the Phoenician-Aryan crew,
translating these stray characters as
"the Briton raised," is sunshine in fog:
the Picts impossible kindred, canceling
all others, but anything they might say lost;
the florid hieroglyphs of imposture
for founding myth.[5] Erasure is real, it is
a road sign painted over, the ground beneath
our feet violently unacquired.
My pamphlet printed by the stationer
enjoys wide circulation in Inverurie:
I have pressed a copy into the minister's
liver-spotted hand, the dust of decades
laid lightly grey against black on his collar.
There is no question of neglect, however
long the stones might hide in earth; your
pretending none of this exists is also
a part of the weather as we gaze across
Pitfichie. I am not bribed by the languor
of incompletion: the stones are speaking now,
the Neolithic vista is the trance
of wandering the back fields and the tang
of all our histories legible on
our double tongues. There remains the permanent
monolith of a world denied: the crystals
in the bloodstream slowed to static; error
triumphant as a dying star still fancied
visible, scarred into granite in our
only language, never spoken here.[6]

5. Alexander Thomson, "Notice of the various attempts which have been made to read and interpret the inscription on the Newton Stone," *Proceedings of the Society of Antiquaries of Scotland* (1865, V).

6. Francis Diack, *The Inscriptions of Pictland* (1944).

A Diurnal Upon St. Lucy's Day

This handful of earth we have selected.
Enter its landscape: you are expected,
and while you drift to sleep, my son,
and dream of the circuit drive you're on,
we leave the village by the bridge
where the Alford railway meets the hitch
of track and bridge both running out;
and wheeping her small circling note
a curlew flies from flooded field
to field in search of reeds and bield.

O Bennachie, Pitfichie and
Cairn William, three wise tors that stand
above the snaking river Don,
and whose stone circles kiss the sun
on solstice mornings when worlds touch
and snowdrifts dazzle, patch on patch:
hem us in against the cold,
poor sheep foregathered in the fold—
who stare like them and see our gaze
returned to us from their blank eyes.

A quarry guards its sunken wound
beyond the pinewood clearance meant
for houses, but left raked and bare:
grant us O Lord our freehold here
and our small hypocrite dissent
when later waves presume to plant
their tarmac lawns of spacious drives,
tailgaters come to live our lives
and multiply the daily round
from village lanes to far-flung town.

Turning for home we hug the wall
of Cluny Castle's darkling pile
and hear the congregated geese,
their heckles pecking at the breeze.
We come, we go, a migrant tide,
our lights are islanded in shade,
the paths we take pure instinct now
as the gritters and the snows allow—
this permanence we grow into,
the passing accident we pass through.

Mr. Green

I'm standing in the doorway trying to zip up my son's coat before we go out, and he is telling me a story about how it was Christmas Eve and "Wibbly Pig was investigating." My fingers are fumbling with the zip-piece and I'm pretty sure he doesn't know what "investigating" means. The coat is green and I will sometimes call him Mr. Green, a label that sticks in my mind even when he's wearing something else, like his less-favored brown coat. I think of how often that other investigator, Wittgenstein, would use the banalest of details, from grinding your teeth to drumming your fingers, to make a point about language, and how we inhabit its protective covering without always knowing what it means, or even what what it means means. If I told you Mr. Green (an actual Mr. Green this time) was wearing a green coat, would you switch mentally from one kind of green to the other while you listened? Suppose you thought accidentally of green the color while saying Mr. Green's name—would that be wrong? We put on and stand inside our words like my son inside his coat. One day we hope to grow into understanding, yet while we wait the coat is still a coat, it still keeps the rain out. Can we go now? For the moment it is I who am holding us up until the zip connects at last. "Ding dong," says my son, though we are closing rather than opening the door. If I could stand here just a moment longer inside the shell of my words, I might unpick this knot of puzzles we carry with us across the park to the café. "Ding dong," he says when we get back, and look, it opens this time, the fresh crumbs of his pancakes smeared round his mouth as his mother comes to the door to scoop him up, Mr. Green, our laughing boy already spilling out of his big billowing coat.

Child Ballad

I Morven Aifric Sadhbh, a child of winter,
doomed to follow where my parents wander,
came unstuck swapping the womb's dark amber
for the paltry welcomes of November.

Mother, father, brother offered comfort
after all that way I'd come for it.
Out of the granite city I was carried
to where that shining silver stone is quarried,

and past the silent playground where I'll test
the reach and grip of infant foot and fist.
My first assertive cries dispersed across
the damp fields mobbed by surly flights of crows.

Dear family, I see that we're alike
if not the same. Whatever I might lack
I claim as mine with busy, grasping hands
untrained for now in telling foes from friends,

but glad to find a yielding breast in reach.
For all your pressing kindnesses I pledge
a stored-up gratitude you may decode
from teenage eyebrows raised and blank eyes rolled.

Whose life grows, whose wilts and falls away?
What waiting futures do my two palms weigh?
What songs you sing me round our daily haunts
will I still know and sing long decades hence?

I see our house is ballasted with junk,
where books accumulate and bookshelves sink.
What trace, tell me, should I hope to add
to all that you have thought and dreamt and said?

I am citizen, not subject, freeborn
daughter of the future I will earn,
yet conscious of the highwaymen that stand
in wait, a loaded pistol in each hand,

and ready to relieve me from the start
of all a girl might need to travel far.
Faces swim from the half-light into view:
are world enough for now, my all, my few.

Nine months I sailed within my mother, now
head up, now down, a fitful questing prow
in search of wider seas. Now you are the tide
I plough, wide world; grant my sails godspeed.

Homage to Inverurie

An odor of dead parents' cleared-out wardrobes
follows us round the charity shop, where I linger
over the vinyl rack between local boys The Steele Combo's
Good Times and Calum Kennedy's *King Of the Highlands*.
"Calum, a former Grampian TV personality of the year,
has established himself in short order as a firm favorite
on the dinner-dance circuit," while "fans in the railway town
are going 'loco' for The Steele Combo's country
and Scottish blend…," and as I browse a delivery
van pulled up outside with a *trompe l'oeil* livery
shunts me off to an edible landscape of grapes and baguette,
much like those I will eat at the Kilted Frog deli-
catessen next door, while—rotating and writhing in the
window seat like fairground ornaments—my children
stare at the facing optician's, taking the eye-test of
their first Scottish market town: which way to the war
memorial, which way to the ogham alphabet embedded
in the footpath down the lane to the music shop,
while two cream legbar hens in a box at the farmers' market
cluck contentedly, their combs flopped over their eyes,
and look out under the eye of our carriage clock of a town
hall for late buses to Methlick, Mintlaw, Macduff.
See Inverurie and die, wrote Arthur Johnston in his best
shire Latin, and if you are planning a funeral, please get
in touch with our friendly, family-run business. Meanwhile
the children scamper between the library and garden center,
the arrival of Thomas the Tank Engine coincides with
the afternoon train from Inverness, and any passengers
alighting in search of slug-repellent or organic manure
would seem to have come to the right place. Ignored
as they go by teens on their lunch breaks, tolerated
by middle-aged shoppers, the children enjoy the cooing

attentions of the charity shops' old ladies, united
in secret knowledge and knowing what only children
and old ladies know: that the decades-long joke starts funny,
goes off in the middle, before getting funny again
somewhere towards the end, that a ticket on an imaginary
railway has no expiry date, and that all this time
the Scotland in Bloom hanging baskets over our heads
have been wreaths and the plastic bags in the shop
doorways patiently awaiting the shirts on our back.

A Compressed Aggregate

for my mother and father

Haze of exhaled quarry-dust
speckling the air over Pitscurry,
and the norite crystals
sparkling in the buzzard's

lucid eye: throaty
lorries loading up in the
works with aggregates
for road-laying, sharp stones

to resurface the decades
since your courting days,
when you inched up the hill past
Calary quarry for Roundwood

to hear Luke Kelly sing—
Oh I've wandered up and
down the world and sure
I've never felt—(my father's

Calary Portakabin
submerged now in the
backfilled pit)—*any surface*
that was equal to the hot asphalt

(my mother's scarf
flying its pennant along
the newly-tarmacked road)—
and afterwards the choice

of the high or the low
road home in the old
Cortina, their long ribbons
tying Djouce and

the Sugarloaf in knots;
miles of rough
country between them,
snaking in parallel

on the leisurely descent,
and then at the end
the two ways coming out
somehow at the same place.

"You found me like a pebble"

after Louis Aragon

You found me like a pebble picked up on the shore
like a strange lost object whose use no one knows for sure
like seaweed on a sextant deposited by the tide
like fog at a window asking only to come inside
like a midden of a hotel room no one has cleaned
the morning after a hooley when the streets and gutters stream
a train traveler bumming a ride sat on the running board
a stream in the field sly river folk have managed to divert
a woodland creature passing cars have frozen in their glare
like a night watchman coming to at the bright dawn hour
like a shady prison dream that morning can't diffuse
like the panic of a bird flapping in the house
like on a lover's finger the signs of a wedding band
the burnt-out shell of a car in some no-man's-land
like a torn-up letter scattered to the four winds
like now summer's flown the tan it's left on your hands
like the glum looks of the lost and the misplaced paths we weave
like the left luggage bags you're planning to retrieve
like when a door or a shutter in the breeze go whack
the furrows of heart and tree alike where lightning's struck
a roadside stone that stands in for the memories we lose
pain that doesn't fade away not like some old bruise
like some boat's vain SOS floated over the waves
like long afterwards the flesh's memory of the blade
like a bolted horse slaking his thirst in a ditch
like a pillow fever-crops of nightmares have bewitched
like an insult to the sky with a straw blindfold on
like fury at there being nothing new under the sun
you found me in the dark like a word reduced to babble
like a vagabond bedded down to sleep in the stable
like a dog with someone else's name on his collar
a man from days of yore full of spleen and choler

Northborough Sonnets

1

Finding John Clare's name carved into a bridge
I pitch our tent for the night no one will
see us from the road but then before dawn
some drunks making a racket uncouth sorts
not safe for a young mother and child try
the next field this goes on for some time then
key to a flat from stranger in pub then
the rent unpaid and a cat left behind
linger in the station ladies' close the
door and lift our feet when the attendant
comes round let ourselves out in the morning
reeking from pools of wee on the floor and
be on our way and whatever you may
choose to remember none of this happens

2

A man on a bicycle come to see
he says his daughter slam door goes away
best keep on the move if they're coming for
us now pin in map and move to northern
town not open door to them either when
they catch up bundling food and clothes through the
letterbox bewildered old couple stood
on the path shouting we know you're in there
grandmother is a very difficult
woman she will stop at nothing to turn
you against me for spite I know she is
watching do not get undressed in front of
the TV letters pile up no money
now but safe where nothing can touch us safe

3

Until fetched home skulking vanquished at bay
mother pushing ninety now cataracts
fogging her view on the drive to the shops
sheer madness but still full of vengeful spleen
don't read in bed barks at me it's a fire
hazard don't think you're having your own front
door key spits while you're under this roof old
so-and-so I keep my enemies close
now wily stratagem I know her game
I am in my childhood bedroom the view
remains the same the woods full of bluebells
hedges full of bloom as the poet wrote
family connection there I fancy
ah blue celeste of poesy counting
the bard's syllables out on my fingers

4

John Clare tracks the placid snipe haunter of
remotest shades marshy flats and stagnant
floods flushes only when approached closely
follows a zigzag course as it takes flight
walk out to Rutland Water and hear it
drumming away to itself mottled brown
and black in the reeds below the osprey
nests and incubating her secretive
revelation that may never take place
soldering the shallows with her needle
bill when the poet moved a few miles up
the road to Northborough his mind darkened
mourning the snipe's peace that in dreariest
places will be a dweller and a joy

5

Mother whose figment of whose mind is who
you do know I'm here don't you unsleeping
your voice carrying entering under
the door is it time for tea yet what are
you doing in there or have you slipped out
on one of your flits again carrying
your things in big heavy bags then slinking
home no acknowledgment and creeping back
upstairs to your hidey-hole yes mother
I hear all unless it is you not there
and who slipped away unnoticed while I
drag out my vigil and scribble my notes
on tissue paper not for reading not
for you mother years of this left long years

6

Going through old family photographs
removing my face emphatic scratching
cancellation of the never happened
or snip you out mother all the photo
cutouts tumbling under the bed into
the archive hand-copied parish records
births deaths marriages long generations
of pig finishers pure collectors their
gammon faces in the tavern gaslight
the ignorant unkillable bloodlines
following me from curtain to curtain
down the village street not seeing me though
not the secret laugh of the struckthrough face
scissored to flitters that pool at my feet

7

Splash damp ground ahead I enter the woods'
marshy acres far from the fruit pickers
on the horizon and the rifle-shots
of the Stamford bus exhaust there is a
clearing where the roots open outwards like
two hands the spew of a low sinky foss
among the flaggy plots investing me
in old sallow stumps unwanted and warped
last-gasp commonage not worth fencing off
I see the sky smile on the meanest spot
and water pooled in my shoes now the damp
leaked in through any old hole stumble on
a brown-black bird tell me its name again
shot drowned in the reeds and its eyes pecked out

Dyspraxia Ode

can you   can you
locate   in a crowded field   locate
        the one thing   necessary

amid the huge   redundancies   of violent effort
        do objects spin   from your grasp
when the drawn   string of   possibility
                tenses   snaps

                did you experience   difficulties
        finding your way here   do you sometimes find
the everyday   impossible

                        experience   a falling short
        in   through   but for which
                the parts of speech   turn like

        wards of a key   in the wrong lock

        these are   my findings

        the lavish kindnesses   of incapacity
humored   fret in the shadow   of a shame

        persistence that leaky tug   sails on a shambles
                wheezing sedition   and the swells beyond
the frosted portholes   follow no trade route

        set course for   no harbor
the jumping horizon   and your seasickness   are one

              howbeit now and then   in the piled wave's shadow
a need is felt   to trace   the pattern
              in the sweat of   a blindness

              to enter   the mouth
of the unspeaking   and know its name

Ellis O'Connor, *West No. 3*

Exploded spray on the sea's glass skull
welled up from lost blank profounds
of eyelessness among the krill
eel beds and orca hunting grounds
would have you feel you cannot feel

how numbly ghosted lines have drawn
the zones of smashed-together wave
and rock the whitened sea-stacks gnawn
and synclines toppled off the graph
of what is measured captured known

by eye improbably afloat
the raft of seeing while the storm
thickens textures into brute
impacted darkness like a charm
to kill all blood-warmth at the root

and opiates of arctic flowers
bob drowned among the sparking shades
of one last glow the evening lowers
to where the deadlight nothing voids
taking me with it disappears

Landscape with Heavy Industry and Washing Line

populate me
animate sensitively
the spirit of dwelling
behind the big blue
harbor storage tanks

I would have
children in animal masks
appearing round lampposts
and knowing the names
of the boats coming in

I desire fishermen
come home to sand-floored
cottages distant factory
boats moored level with
the breakwater wall

my life has been
a series of sailors' knots
tightened and loosed
stronger than floodtides
and briefly-lingering

traceries across
my palm where the blood
knot and perfection loop
have slipped through
my fingers

I have hung out
the laundry in front
of the house on the Sabbath
and had it back through
the letterbox I have had it

with all but
the ship in a bottle
the scene becomes sooner
or later the heaped rigging
unfurled

with a yank
on a string and the whole
salty tale set down
and forgotten between
lace curtain and window.

Aberdeen Elegy

A marijuana whiff over the graves
off Union Street, where lunchtime dossers lounge,
ourselves among them, packs a fetid punch
as foghorns sound and a hungry scurry reives
for chipbag, fag-end, any old dreck really.
Here among flax-spinner's tombs, shipmasters',
nameless children lost to small disasters,
the spirits of the sun-becalmed might rally.
Old stones where weeds show through are green but barren,
grey but quick with a warmth they somehow catch.
Just don't expect much more than a yawn and stretch,
the sluggish self-delight of a ring-pull's pop
from a cemetery paved with bodies, and a bairn-
in-arms drifting awake from a midday nap.

One Door May Conceal Another

Les rois ne touchent pas aux portes. – Francis Ponge

It is the month of May: you open
and you close; you open and close
the door, the press, a small plastic
replica of the house. You bring
to the unappeasable destruction
of small towers the ambling gait
of a watchful gunslinger
tumbled smack to the floor.
For that he starteth and leapeth
and boundeth with jubilation,
thinks the tabby cat hunched
alarmed-faced at your feet.
You slide the glass door open and
surprised but pleased see
your face swim into place
on another behind it. Walls
are doors, shifting tectonic
plates of the open and closed,
the way in and out. Imagine
the sadness of kings never
touching doors for themselves
or uncovering with small
anemone fingers trailed round
the edge of the door their faces.
Face waiting all that time
to emerge from behind
your mother's and mine, there
is the you behind the door
and the you that comes through it
in search of a book full of
moving parts. You open the book
and shrieking splay-fingered
brace your open arms with the
thrill of this, just this, this here.

Dear Cliff Forshaw

All I want is a view
of the river from your studio
in sluggish oils—
do the swallows still dip
over the mudbanks as though
draping bunting from mill to mill?
the mudbanks gravid
with—what was the word—
lutulence—
Latinate sparkle
on so much absorptive
unregeneracy and we two
very much sunk in it—
I saw a brick impacted there
in a window like those
troublesome wisdom teeth
I left behind in Hull—
at such cross purposes with my gums—
perhaps that Christmas when
confounding the flat-lining streets—
like walking on the seabed
Douglas Dunn said—
some unfortunate took
a header from the top
of the mill by the swing-bridge—
and we saw as we passed
how they'd cleared
the snow from the pavement
where he fell—
where the meltwater run-off—
"those watery lines and plummets"—
coursed down the drains

of Marvell's Wincolmlee
surveyed by you now
from the top of your tower—
a view I see streaked
not just with the mud
of the Hull's banks but
the clabbery mud in my eye

Portrait of a Man Thought
to be Andrew Marvell

As one put drunk into a Humber keel
taking his chance on high tide's surge and swell,
though soaked through I feel my palms grow clammy
at the thought of Winestead sliding from me.
My mind is sand, the channels that it tills,
the mazy, secret kingdoms that it builds.
Albion's high towers in shadow now
infesting prelates their dark plumage show,
until a man might keep a blade concealed
about himself for who knows what dark need.
Such a man as "Mr. George," who crossed
with me to Holland on some special tryst
and pressed on me a pamphlet much inclined
to warnings on fair liberty's decline.
Nameless men I meet in coffeehouses
keep their wide brims pulled down on their faces
riddling where the root of power might lie,
in pope or potentate — or must it die
if not for their great secret work in hand?
The lords at home will learn of what they plan.
Take signs for wonders. Apocalypse engulfed
the great gunpowder keg one day in Delft.
I saw a finch land stunned on a wall-bracket:
the fabric of reality had cracked
and I gone through it. My alias grown vague,
I meet a king in waiting in the Hague
(whose name it is not politic to share),
in whom are wed divine right and forced power.
The man once "thought to be Marvell" purses
his lips at all these tragedies and farces,
and "Mr. George" picks up a little Dutch

for use at cards, the fishhouse, or at church,
and opening new channels of accord
to pass on what the lords at home report.
But whose will be the kingdom still in shade,
the guests for whom the still-life feast is laid?
The battle scenes show how the navy warred,
the faces on the frigates faint and blurred,
but a girl with a lute or posed with a terrier
unseals the space of an interior:
strange privacies reclaimed like a polder
from an outgrown frame that cannot hold her,
and I, unmoored whether I leave or stay,
feel the ground shift and England slip away.

In Search of the Tenderer Thorns

Wait for the change in the tide where the Ouse meets the Trent and the Humber is born. Sound your foghorn once and slip down the jetty, where a tethered goat flicks its ears in the breeze and skitters a volley of piss in your general direction. These parishes, their runneled fields all alluvial warping and tillage, secrete their tidal glue round your feet, and the scabby-legged cockerels in the bend of the road have spied you, Phrygian caps a red shock of rebellion. Follow them twice round the mulberry bush and into the churchyard: follow the late poet squire of Yokefleet's cigarette tip in the distance like a will o' the wisp across the "fructuant marsh," and stumble into the arms of a barman out beating the bushes on pressgang duty for the Tuesday night darts team. Stand everyone at the Hope & Anchor a drink, and that grass, that mistcircled grass on the dyke, cock an ear for its whisper under the jukebox and the farm dog barking half a mile down the road. That island out in the estuary, what is its name, the island out where the freighters pass and the avocet dips and wades: it's a trick of perspective, you're on the island, you're in the nature reserve, you're already drifting out to sea with the estuary mud; there is no island and never was, the goat has progressed to chewing its tail, you slip back on board, sound the foghorn again and disappear into the chaos beyond the last high tide. And a couple of pound coins in the change, thanks, for the condom machine in the jakes, and a packet of crisps. Where the Ouse meets the Trent and the Humber is born, that swaying grass, that mistcircled grass.

2000s

In Stranraer

The diesel generator's
chug we feel through the walls
is not the morning sailing
but a rumbling come from
deep in the earth, a pulse
in search of a wrist.
Last night with my back
to the sea I dreamt of the lorry
traffic like migrant birds,
seasonal and singing
to one another at dawn.

On the dry side of the long
curved shore this is a town
for the land-locked too,
the girl who walked to work
in the dark and is sorry
but there is no margarine,
the chef on his break
sitting smoking on your
window-ledge in the yard.

Never leave, say
the plastic flowers in the vase:
the ferry port cannot
forgive the boats and back-
packers hardly knowing
where they are off to.
What is it, though, biding
its time at the sky's fitful edge
we so distrust, its grey at once
ashen and incendiary?

Wanting his grog
Old Bill Barley, retired
ship's purser, pounds
on the floor with a blackthorn
in the guesthouse crow's nest,
retching up green gobbets
as though from the ebb-
tide's backwash.

Raising himself on one
elbow he reaches under
the sheets for a telescope
and trains it on the Belfast
ferry. Unless he watches it
all the way to the horizon,
long study has taught him,
the boat isn't sailing, it will
just hang there lifeless all day.

To Lough Tay

Can I come in asks
the cat at the door at this
or that but always the same
one door regardless where
on this earth we have
dragged her behind us.

Lough Tay old Wicklow
puddle can I come in
again enter your waters
where a cat might fish
by trailing a hand in
these these and these

small elsewheres
the mill-pond over
the hill the mackerel's
back of a loch seen
from the car, cold waters
breaking against what

far foreign shore.
A goat scales your sheer
basin Lough Tay and
falling the scree rebounds
over the waves to rattle
around the skull

of whoever is there
and my skull too.
Slow but at last delayed
echoes of blank-eyed
Wicklow goats on
the move reach me

and the skin of that
thin umbrella memory
blowing off lands
again in the over-
flown well of your
crinkled blaze of light.

Flags and Emblems

homage to Tom Paulin

Are they part of us asked
the man in the post office

of the Northern Irish fiver
the shopper crinkling

his Queen in his palm
I looked to the woman

in the queue but it wasn't
her place any more

than mine to comment
our awkward wee moment

as Irish as Larkin's
souvenir UVF tie

the Larne gun-runners
paid no import duty

queued for no stamps
it was free trade of a kind

or is that Southern Ireland
the postmaster added

somewhere anyway
in need of a cloot

to wipe itself down
from the bustit sewage

tanker fornenst the diamond
in Crossgar the week of

the vote randomly
spraying clabbery glar

and shite everywhere
not much of a metaphor

granted in a world where—
gable-ends curbstones

Brexit—things mean
themselves and nothing

besides and you can't
clean up shite that's

still spraying and clagging
the eyes in your head

and but for the flags on
the lampposts you'd hardly

know what country it was.

Mouth Music

i.m. Ciaran Carson

It's on the island over my shoulder
over the minch that I was born

the crooked-horned ewe was on the rock
and would not let a soul approach

that elegant and cantankerous ewe
whose wool grew the color of grass

the speckled hen we had that time
is away inside a thief's coat now

and the churl who married the goose girl
is drunk before noon or saying his prayers

when I was young and on the island
it's she who was along with me

and there would be dancing after snuff
and cards of a night in Murdo's house

I used to sing and when I did
like all good singers spoke not sang

the final line wrongfooting any
dancers full of wild bravado

convinced as how could they not be there
was still that little bit left to come

Our Lady of the Snows

When the redcoats took Corgarff they found
the fire still lit, a cat on the hearth-rug,

and piled-up snow in an open window looking
over the pass. There are places whose task

it is to turn their backs and watch for what
we miss in the sunken market towns far

from the prowling fox. Lady Campbell,
watching the horizon, *thocht it was*

her ane dear laird that she saw ridin hame,
before firing off a pistol when

she learned her mistake. In no time
the castle had burned to the ground.

Only when seen from above does the walls'
star-shape come into view, hardest and least

forgiving of snowflakes. Lost in thoughts
of St. Martin, who shared his cloak

in a snowstorm, I pulled onto the verge
before noticing the other driver

was in fact the Queen. At the chapel
found at last down a dirt-track, slush-

colored hens ran free in the open door
on the shortest day of the year. When

we speak of lost histories it is real
bodies we mean, one regiment melting

into another in the glen, a hind
looking over her shoulder at the sound

of gunfire, and on my tongue the absent
wafer of the snow that was not falling.

Child Ballad

An outlandish knight came from the Northland
fox in the fields and red kites on the hill
Easter come and the snow down still
to sleep in the arms of his lady fair

the yard end that evening stood droukit and bare
the burn still flowing under the ice
he's courted you once and courted you twice
and stretched out to you his little white hand

he's crossed the hillside on his laird's dark mare
haunting the woods by the old sheepfold
daunering towards us across the pine-cones

to win the hand of his lady fair
not shivering though who does not feel the cold
but carries it unlike us in his bones

The Bothy at Tillyfourie

after Montale

Mind thon bothy in Tillyfourie, between
the quarry and the disappeared railway,
in whose empty window your thoughts
took refuge like an incongruous candle
lit for nothing and no one. North-
westerlies down from the mountains

licked at the walls for years
like jaded paws on a cat-flap,
while the heart went out of your laughter;
the compass is an unhinged spinning wheel
and one throw of the dice abolishes chance.
Your memory's smudged to a blank
by the past's return, and the thread unravels.

I still hold one end, but the house
shrinks in the distance and the smoke-
blackened weathervane points without pity
this way and that. I hold one end, but
altogether elsewhere you are alone,
not breathing co-conspiratorially into my darkness.

Oh, that flickering plumb-line of the horizon!—
round every corner and none in the hills—
where the tanker's lights blink through the smirr:
is that where I cross, where the foam
scuds and rants as the cliffs fall away?
Coming and going we swap places,
and I don't know anymore who's who.

Wolf Girl, Clais Mhadaidh

                                I sense
                    it is you
from the bothy door's rattle:

        could it have been
a mistake   to leave your name   on the map
        all this time?

        I have known you   from the gamekeeper's tale
of the cailleach   meeting you   in the lane with
        a gridiron to hand

and when my father sent me   up the drove road
with a seedcake   and file   I knew the shadow

        of your permission would fall   across my path
somewhere between   restoration
        and the irremediable

        where was a pack   was a trail
is a trail still   noun-verb   you conjugate
        where you brush   with a reconsecrated
        dew claw   the alpine milk-vetch   again

and where   does the first   fresh footprint go
        landing as though   out of the sky?

        a pelt's   unfinished business
leaves its story   .   neither   drowned in the burn
        nor on the lodge wall

and tracking your   shadow incautiously   I find
           an odor   of old peaty hags
of a nip of Scotch   taken in the fauld   of a morning

but will you turn   to disregard   me over a shoulder
        as you slope into   the spruce cover
under the ravenous   drench of   an August dawn

where I think of myself   in the light of extinction
        name   habitat   behaviors
passing hidden into   the fossil record

        except I can't bring you back
                    all I do is
toss your echoing passage   round the high corrie
            walls of the hollow
wearing your name   like a spider-web
        beaded with frost

and grasping   like a palmful of haar   that

        there are some thoughts   these
can be thought only   between
        a girl and   her wolf

The Fourth Craw

i.m. *Roy Fisher*

I am driving the Jacobite army north from Derby.

Three craws sat upon a wa

You can go there if
you want, into that past,
all banners and ballads,

and lie in its grievance
shaped to a vacancy.
I remember the trampling

of the flag, and a horse,
legs gone, catching
its tail as it fell.

The first craw was greetin fer his maw

Assigning legs and arms
to this or that body
among the tangle

balletic tableau

I watched the sun-
light cross the valley

merciless but gilding
our profiles fondly

as we took flight.

The second craw fell and broke his jaw

Living that high up
said the woman in the courtyard

holding my reins and
gesturing over the hills

anywhere else must
feel like a comedown

so many worlds
of patient neglect

stored up for our
return and whose

forgiveness
won't come cheap.

The third craw couldna flee awa

Following by night
the ginnels and shambles of Leeds

as though a blind man should trace
with his fingers the features

of a child's face
we came to the North

good enough to have
stayed where we left it

And the fourth craw wasna there at aa

the ways closed over
behind us and all manner

of joyous lament finding
its proper dark at last.

Poem beginning with line spoken by a toddler

        The noise is in my hair
as morning unfreezes   the red kite's *weoo-weoo*
        paused overnight   on the wing

a line of yew trees   falls to its knees

        the light in   the closed-up house
where we pick apples   flickers
        on and off   sensor

or panic   of bewildered age
        a shuttered eye   too late to harvest
                the residual   manifest

        a blackbird sings   in the hollow
of the hand   I raise to the tree
        a gust of wind   appears   to lift
the cinderpath   under our feet

        O leafy October
                          sycamore wildfire
it's you   I'm wild for

and lifting my daughter   for a view of
        a heron descending   I find
I have framed her   standing tall
        on the other bank

Paysage moralisé

découvrant la clairière les ailes s'effacent
c'est la lune qui revêt un lieu de détresse
une cécité qui me dévisage de partout
l'ombre qui penche d'un vieux hibou
les formes qui flambent au creux de la nuit
le bois peint en argent amer et gris
c'est à peine si je respire cette nuit trop lourde
j'enlève le sommeil mais la brume je la garde
de l'inconscient un hublot mi-clos
qui se noie et s'efface sans bruit dans l'eau
il y a des feux féroces qui s'éteignent
tout le long des hautes montagnes
et qu'est-ce que j'entends immobile sinon
mes pas inquiets qui glissent et s'en vont

Immigrant Song

Standing on top of a mountain our children
look back over the sea for the country
whence their parents traveled in search of
imagined faraway mountains, from which

to look back over the sea for the country
that said, there was nothing for them there—
imagined faraway mountains where
the present sees the past reflected

and says, there is nothing for you here
to the cracked, distorting mirror
where the past sees the present reflected,
and past and present's two streams cross

in the cracked distorting mirror
of a mirage-afflicted view:
past and present's two streams crossed,
one mountain reformed to another;

a mirage-afflicted view
opening, closing on the future,
one mountain reformed to another
twice over, but which is which?—

where opening, closing on the future
we turn here and there inside out
twice over—but which is which?—
and sink one country into the other,

here and there turned inside out
by our children on top of a mountain
sinking one country into another
and us, not here yet, traveling towards it.

Granite Elegy/Dàn do Eibhir

Buchan is harrowed ● the Cabrach lies empty.
The shepherd stands in ● the church's chevroned door
watching it multiply ● regressing arch
by arch to the roofless ● sacrament house
where a hare has sat out ● the wars of religion. On no
monument then or now ● the unnamed missing
follow the drove roads ● downhill where
the burn has scored ● the face of the Old Mill.

At the turn on the high ● road I pass through
myself on the way ● in and there is
a hole, a war-time ● lid in the earth where
the landscape hid ● slow-smoldering while
the planes flew over ● The invention
of steam-powered ● cutting had transformed
the memorial industry ● the shining stones
glittered upright in the ● earth as never before.

So many departures ● under that hidden sun;
incurious, I am not ● looking for what
I have found but ● at the summit happen on
three carved, interlocking ● fish out of water,
a guestbook for the ● open air tucked
under a rock ● (a vacated throne)
and single capsules ● of green shield-moss
blowing on all sides ● sprouted from nowhere.

Here is a land where • nothing is settled
these thousands • of years. When Christ
came to Scotland • the oystercatchers
helped conceal him • under some seaweed
until his enemies • passed. The unmelting
snow patch I know • is there is hiding under
some snow, a glacier • as thick as my need
for a last recess beyond • the reaching palm.

Over the ages piled high • like a cairn my steps
persist through the • granite blizzards in the
direction of patience • while I number the peaks
like antler tips where • the damp moss gathers.
Now I stand in a fold • on the map glutted
on horizons to come • a mouse in its claws
where the Buck opens • the two huge shrouds
of its flanks and falls • on me from the sky.

A Pine Wood in North Africa

I am in a great hurry. Could you keep this for me until this war is over?
  —Sorley MacLean to Douglas Young, September 25, 1939

Among El Alamein's
reversing dunes a pinewood
of the mind walks the shifting
ridge whispers rumors to
its roots of a waterhole
and rings with a great music
of helmets hammers banners
of the great wood in motion
in the scirocco, the divided
wood bright with the brightness
of the face remembered
in the phosphorescent
night of another sky.

Under another sky
the ringing of exploded laughter
and the creak of the opening graves
to salute the men departed
and welcome the men returned
the wounded Actaeon
bleeds on the sand and slowly
brain and heart converge
on one belief; it is the depths
from which they climb
that burden the mountains so
and the sap is known as it oozes
rising to its proper work.

Dear Douglas in the event
of my death preserve
my poem on the pinewood
watching over this sandy
foxhole file away in an
airless drawer its branches
and their steely shadows
sweating under a cloudless
sky and keep in your breast
pocket the needles I stooped
to gather once in a musky
handful somewhere Scotland and this
waiting desert met and touched.

A Sconser Tartan

In front of the landscape
I hear the saint's bell's
insular echoes pooling
round Loch Sligachan
and weaving peal by
peal their tartan prayer.

Floated over the loch
I see Dùn Caan in the white
zone, stitched from
a Raasay cloud, the snow
in its veins coursing through
my peaty encampment.

I see the sheer burns
rush backwards in
the blanketing winds and
rise up spuming into
my face, Allt Garbh
Beag and Allt Garbh Mòr

coursing down from
the white to the grey
and the grey to the purple,
the yellow, the green,
the brown, parts of a world
for my slow deciphering.

In front of the landscape—
the mobile, unraveling
features rolled into
place then off on their
travels, carrying with them
the map as they go:

orphaned shapes
of indefinite memory
weaving their tartan
prayer on the loom
of a landscape they will
thread through your eyes.

Reliquary

Monymusk: a pillaged
world and its treasures;
a saint's bones stashed
in a rattling lunchbox

borne into battle under
the seal of a beast on
a painted field and biting
her tail. I would lay

in the empty reliquary
the ghost of reverences
to come as I bear my child
aloft by the river, gift

sufficient unto himself
whatever he chooses
to carry of me through life
be it something or nothing

Souterrain

Les siècles aussi vivent sous terre
    – Henri Michaux

All day through a telescope
I watch the archaeological dig
tunnel through the skyline
on Bennachie's floating summit
where a souterrain bricked up
under a ring-fort has
surfaced for air.

Our houses too are stacked
along a hill, so that our
sleeping heads lie somewhere
under our neighbors' feet,
and our eyes are drawn
upwards by the postman's
tread making off down the street.

Amid a clatter of quern-
stones hauled above ground
I feel us shedding layer
upon layer of fine dust,
swimming towards a rarer
sky in the May evenings
of light without end

when I brace waking against
what should be dark
on my pillow, draining
into the earth now,
leached from the swallow-
kissed eaves where
the shadows should go.

A Clashindarroch Wildcat for Tom Pickard

What to infer
from the coarse
        fur left
on barbed wire

        do I scratch do I
        hiss do I spit

in the gleed of the gorse
        and the harebells what
to learn from the scat

        in the slack
by the braeheid
        sheep-bucht
                steid

so much sky as will
        hardly fit
and me low
        to the yird

how do you want
        my extinction event
picturesque or
        with blood on the snow

        who coming
on my own spoor
        think only
to lowp and attack

teeth smeared
          with gralloch
tail fanned before
          jinkin awa

if I'm here at
          all and that skirl
from the woods is
          not some other
          night-beast's call

flitting to where
               I bicker
          and hide and long-

          outbred but with
an itch still to scratch
               breed out

so that I
          am the tart whiff
          your house-cat
trails through the flap

and rather these
          reiver's raids
          than a gloved hand
filching my spunk

into tube or vat
and your eyes on mine
          and no bolt-
hole in sight

till I blend with the feral
		tom you'd kill
for my sake
		killed in his place

		in the name of
the ultimate trace
		of what
intangible shadow

I cast over
		your disgrace
that I hiss to scorn

in the cranreuch
		come down
like a shroud of glass
		over the burn

and nothing and no
		one sees
		my face ·

Stanzas for a Lover

after Donnchadh Bàn Mac an t-Saoir

Not for you the wisp
as love charm or water from straws
but reeling in the one
you're stuck on and no mistake

Up with you on the smooth
flagstones early on Sunday
gather handfuls of butter-
bur and monkshood
and carry them with you
on your shoulder in
a small wooden scoop

Cut with an axe
nine stalks of bracken
take from a grave
three bones of a bodach
burn on a kindling fire
and reduce to ashes

Rub on your love's white
breast while facing into
a stiff north wind and I warrant
he'll see you right

To the River Don

We came to a bend
        in the river
                where

a willow washed
        its hair in its
                double

and tangles of
        geese shadows
                shrank

to a stickleback
        tide passing
                under

the bridge so that
        the reeds sprouted
                eyes

in which here
        too our reflections
                swam

and do they feel
        themselves
                changing

direction
    the fish or is
        whatever

way the tide
    goes merely
        the way

Gaelic Lane Elegy

dead men's	ùird
hammers	nam marbh
sculpting	a' snaidheadh
Christ to his	Chrìosd gu a
cross with	chrois le
insular care	cùram-tìre
the nails	na tarragan
and flesh	agus an fheòil
of one substance	a' measgachadh
their kirk	còmhla
an upside-	an eaglais na
down quarry	cuaraidh bun
while they	os cionn
its makers	's an luchd-togail
withdraw	'a falbh airson
to their islands	nan eilean
and leave	's an dìleab
as memorial	mar chuimhneachan
great gaps in	beàrnan mòra sa
the landscape	dealbh-tìre
filled in	gan lìonadh air
lest we suspect	eagal gun ionnsaich

what the earth	*sinn na gheall*
once promised	*an talamh*
and tremulous	*agus*
slow surge	*an ataireachd*
of petrified	*slaodach clachach*
grace that	*de ghràs*
it is	*a thèid*
delivered	*lìbhrigeadh*

Alteration

i.m. *Derek Mahon*

Sunt aliquid manes. You'll know the line—
polite fiction the dead and living talk.
O clock hands ticking out your time and mine,
the self-subtracting hours they gave and took:
words inch youwards but still want to know
which version of you they are talking to.

Come in from or accept again the cold.
I struck out for the nearest snow-fringed field,
following where a high, lone osprey called.
I tried to try your shadow on and failed.
My down, not feathers, was made less for flight
than an earthbound vertigo that's all my fault.

Your dandy's arcs and feints on high insist
there are places still the suave marauder
makes his cozy own. But Kinsale is lost:
the routed earl has crossed the silvered water,
the lone grey tidal breach that marks your passage
and no reflux can seal up or assuage.

The infinite changes and what stays the same
is that one point where options all run out.
I see the osprey, claws first, spin, take aim,
dive remorseless and first time get it right.
The trick is less to alter than dissolve
all forms now dead that do not salve or solve.

Three Ponies

Under the beak of a jet overhead
and the boom of the aftermath it's shed
we choose the woodland path up over
the far field where the kestrels hover
until indignant hoarse and stiff
the bigger buzzards drive them off.
The wood anemones have pushed
up by the path where newly lush
a line of mossy tree stumps teems
with aphids fresh-hatched from their seams
in search of tangy beech-nuts spread
on the spongy carpet that we tread.
An old felled pine trunk from last winter
flaunts its taproots disinterred
and here no higher than my face
a wren's nest coories in its base.
High in Leschangie's woodland attic
sat in the lee of an old erratic
we watch where the yellow wagtail trots
and count the wee reid-sodgers' spots
until small skittish feet announce
that on we'll press to further haunts.
And where they wander slip and prang
we shepherd-coax the pair along
who touch we too but only via
these two small bodies in our care
and as I fall behind two deer
hurdle the low fence and land square
in my path inquiring Who goes there?
before they turn and disappear.
And as we climb to higher ground
we come to a clearing like a mound

outsoaring lowly cares and griefs
its grassy clumps like unmarked graves.
But even here companionship
's a short trot off across the slope
to where three ponies holding court
smack their lips and gamely snort.
Fond beasties lined up spine to spine
they groom each other tightly twined
even if I can't but wonder
if sometimes they don't pull asunder
who nip and tug and yank their fill
eyes wilder all the while until
a single view is hard to form
of what is care and what is harm.

Chiaroscuro

A torch on his head the jogger in the park
swims up from the coalface of the dark.
Abroad before the bloodless winter sun
I scan the black for tears through which leak in
a street sweeper's lemon high-viz glow,
late Christmas lights left on all night for show.
Yet dark is the element that holds me close,
still pregnant with the hedgerows' morning calls
below bare trees that keep guard as we sleep
and wait now to assume a daylit shape.
Not once but twice around the block careers
an early bus to rev up work-day cares
with every jolt for folk who're nae sae braw
after the fug of last night's last hurrah.
A tractor idles by the Co-op while
a dog is tethered by its monstrous wheel
but you remain where I left you swaddled tight
inside the duvet's latibule of night,
breath mingled in the chill with our twa bairns
while arse flap-slapped a vagrant cat returns.
And I in the dark am exposed to all that comes,
night fears at large till morning coffee calms.
So where am I bound but where a stove is lit
and the outline daylight draws draws up a seat.
The chiaroscuro of a half-drawn blind
leaves light and darkness made, remade, entwined
as day admits me like a watched-for omen,
the café door swung wide with a hoarse "Come in."

Long Slide

I am galumphing round the soft-play center
like something from Brueghel the Elder's *Peasant Wedding*,
all food-stained flapping jumper and odd socks,

conjoined boisterously with the toddler I carry
like bagpipes and locked in a tuneless, circling dance
with fellow parents and their flailing loads.

Flemish weddings could go on for rather a long
time, celebrations stopping only to restart,
and after enough circuits the child in your arms

may morph into another, just as a first pancake
may lead to a second. It is unclear where the husband
in Brueghel's painting has wandered off to,

or if he is present at all. But I am distracted,
the toddler has crawled away, and a war-cry from
the play tower and slide has me fearing the worst

before her emergence swamp-monster-like
from the colored balls pit, and I am reminded there is
in fact no wrong way to go down that slide.

Two from Reverdy

CURFEW

A nook at the end of the world offers shelter
the columns of evening strain
and the door opens onto the night
a single lamp keeps vigil
at the end is a wonder
of unknown heads
and on the wall dissimilar maps
my face more erased
between us the warm trembling air
        a faded memory
between the four peeling walls
        no one speaks
the fire goes out under the smoke

BETWEEN TWO WORLDS

        A shadow capers
        nothing but the self-
        threshing wind remains
movement spreads and dilates
        from the wall

there are souls born
for an instant or for eternity
in the mutable night alone
        with someone remorse-gnawn
me to one side
on the road where his step falls·
        and nothing can be seen of what is

below the louring wall
      a sign from my heart extends to the water
      no one can stop the earth rolling over
worn out by movement and thrawn
while a blue star above turns upside down

The Enigma of Arrival

Which way you turn at the entrance
means more than this or that
trail of pictures there is no time
to look at, however slowly you walk—
and how could the glances not know that,
you think, checking over your shoulder.

The woman behind the glass dwells
on a middle name to make talk,
and another beside you asks
again when told there's nothing
you want, as though coffee
cups were for more than clutching.

Wandering the corridors you start
down a dead-end with a high, round window,
more like a porthole, sit to recover
yourself where the light might go
on a Spring day, and supply a pier
sliding past on the Belfast ferry
while you tense and wait for the call
to go down to the bright, thronged hold.

Glow

for Molly

Be the flower that holds on late,
montbretia, as October storms —
orange-red the bells that shake
and orange-red the flame that warms.

Where the spilt ink of the dark
comes for us over evening's hills
root in shelter your quick spark
from which illumination spills.

Orange of the bonfire night,
pool of your eyes in which it glows,
preserve the small montbretia shoot
where what summer made still grows.

Flower that crowns you as you trace
a path through hazard, find a way
to draw together in one place
all that stays and does not stay.

Line-Breaks

Snaking down the valley
home with practiced
leanings-in to the cross-
stitched road, fifty now
and licensed to wonder
how many more of these
autumns await
stored up to fringe
the windscreen with future
frost: owl on the wing
keeping pace with the car;
low sun full in my eyes
and me on a whim bouncing
the question against
the bends as I go, the
merest sensation of
batting it this way, that
way, this way, that way.

Marriage

In a house not ours with no back
door I stared from an upstairs
window while you among wind-
tossed rags of pewits tripped
over furrows down to the river
and the nameless islands lapped
by serene, unnavigable tides.

I too tripping over bare
floorboards, raised and missing,
framed our son in the window
of the preserved abandoned
child's room I'd found, as he
stood and gazed the length of the river
to where there could only be sea.

All of us looking towards
the mountain we planted our steps
with care in search of the one
shared lucky foothold somewhere
between the shell of a life
abandoned and the whole
implacable summer to come.

A Return

A silence all out of tune
where a window frames the moon
steps absorbed in the moss
of a threshold I would cross

where the floorboards crack and rot
of a house with no door to lock
and clay in the stripped-out grate
is the wind's to sift and lick

I come with a word on my lips
that the damp air chills and stops
a question I'd meant to ask
trampled into the grass

as I call from the outside in
and instead of an answer find
only a dark bedded down
whose are the echoes that sound

when did the truth of a house
become what's left not what leaves
where I poke a toe into lives
laid in fresh ashes but whose

Un/Settled

arrived
from impoverished   distance unpacked
a country   my daughter has
never seen   called her own
our current of life   diverted
unbidden   from that flow
and a migrant   tongue stitched
to the cheek   so as
to live   un/settled
in the permanence   of the other
to follow a patch   of rainbow light
across a sliding   glass door
in one of life's   upstairs corners
      where the concealed   tracks have
led me too   under a skyline
only I   drawing the curtains   find
      myself here   to hold up
pinned at dawn   above   the line of trees
this land I have watched   for decades now
whose guilts only   the migrant knows
tidy calamities of sunsets   tossed
westwards   over my shoulder

Зеркала

Who am I now,
Leschangie hill, in
the shifting mirror of
memory: father or child?
I fell behind on the forest path
to frame us at large among pines
and spruce, and seeing you wander
thought of reciting something—
Russian for preference—
"our path was through forget-
me-nots and wild dog roses,
I wore no coat, words clung
like leaves to the trees..."—
following where a village doctor
might traipse over fields to treat
a consumptive or a soldier home
from the wars. Sodden
beneath shrugging conifers
I stumbled on a tree root
where we stopped to read
A Midsummer Night's Dream
and feast on berries
(it is a pleasure to fall down
with an attractive woman)—
wild berries, their over-ripe joy
clasped in a baby's hand
to burst against the palate
in blood-red streams. Over
the hill lay the sunken mill-
pond and tumbledown
bothy—domino sets
of tadpoles spilled on the large

flat stones under the algae,
half-sunk cement bags
agape in the breeze, and
a tractor tire drowned in its lining.
Already day was burning
up the horizon along
the line where clouds and hay-
ricks met and a barn in a far
field was a furnace reflected;
then coming down the other
side we moved into shadow and
reached the old factory where
a cat colony ate from sauce-pans—
a three-legged black cat
darting over the hot stones
like a dropped glove
carried off in a breeze.
I peered through a window
and saw cascades of indoor
rain on abandoned post
and where the plaster had fallen
in lumps, outdoors trying
to get in and indoors trying
to get out, before we sat in
an overgrown windowless
fire-engine and felt fresh moss
at our feet. Already awash,
the zone was an overflow
of prodigal roots, burns,
buds and berries. Yet even
now I was already home and
feeding the scene through

the mirror, watching the ceiling
under the sky come down
and with it a plashy drenching:
the children scooped in our
arms and off up the hill
while I reeled in the mill-pond,
the buzzards and harebells
tucked into a ruck-sack
pocket. The glassy white discs
are honesty, the snowberries
fit just so between a fleeing
child's finger and thumb,
their palms more daring and
lighter than birds. Sodden,
she too, the children's mother
shakes out her hair through
the raindrop lens of my gaze,
too much immediacy wiped
away like the downpour from
my eyes, and the laughter
among the trees still coming
after us down the path,
following what can only
have been the right way home.

A Curious Herbal

Mushrooms could grow on a person all the same
  – Ailbhe Darcy

honor to Leschangie
        unknown
among braes winner
        of no renown

but spot where
        at our child's toe
heath-rush and deer's-
        hair grass grow

bruchorachd is cìob
        herbs that bring
strength

        rust-brown sorrel
and rye grass too
        cuiseagan is riasg

the small red blooms
        wind-pollinated
where seeds blow

        primrose
St. John's wort
        and tormentil flowers

        sòbhrach 's eala-bhì
's barra neònagan

as the bough lowers
        and the sun's balloon
comes down again

on the spotted orchid's
         dance of the hours

                 dóbhrach bhallach mhìn
ghóbhlach bharrach
         shlìom

petals proferred and
         withdrawn

         one language
darkening into
         another's gleam

              ★

"flower name here"
         sketching a poem
awaiting our daughter's

         birth I stalled
not knowing what
         I was looking at not

having looked at what
         I could see and left
a placeholder for

clump of montbretia
         by the barn door
bright orange torch

         a summer gorsefire
cone of light
         on a ginger cat's back

unsuspecting
       the place I held with
my flowering blank

was yours child
       in bloom who
knows flowers'

       names and tells them
pointing

       what's that one
daddy   *what is it*

      ★

fresh to the mycelial
       carpet and feeling
the cords quiver

       at her tread here
then is your two-
       year-old botanist

coming just over
       your knee and all
the closer for that

to the scatter
       and spread of
penny buns and

harebells where her
       quick steps lead

grazing heifer with
      necklace of fern
threaded with speedwell—

      that rock-plant
invader
      nicknamed
Veronica

      who mopped
Christ's brow—

      and bush vetch
scrambling perennial
      more at home
in the roadside

grit your steps
      churn
daughter and where

you call
      over the fence
cow   cow

    *

where the path ended
      a tire mountain spitting

in drizzle behind
      the dairy sheds

votive hecatomb
      fuming untended

*

beech bark fungus
the one bright
        thing

in the winter
        wood

prising ajar
        a trunk where
beech scale-

        wounds sprout
and redcoat rot
        runs riot

where faded and
        failed now
all that was summer
        stood

        *

        where an oak
has fallen high

        in Leschangie
amethyst deceivers

        Plutonically
purple and blue

        gather "the
daytime torchlike"

                and drain
as it grows late

                in the year
their glow

                from where
"Demeter's pale lamps

                give off light"

                ★

dark now at
half-past three
what
                sub-arctic

of the mind
is this
                we inhabit
split off and
                glacially adrift
like an
                erratic

                ★

Beauty: impurities in the rock (Niedecker)

December sun's
Winterreise
                circuit
of despair

         briefly
paused on the
              granite
standing stone's

splash of
            jasper

            ★

soil as under-
              earth skyline
for patches of fairy clubs
              poking through

secretive army
              weapons raised
against our footsteps'
              thundering blast

              we who are
in all ignorance but
              the clouds of their
sky scudding past

            ★

rocks are flowers
slowed down
              rocks' blood
courses through
flowers' veins

but bloodless and cold
mushrooms shun
the sun
      are having none
of our floribund ways

      bide their time
children of dark
to break down—

      our days
on earth done—
      the children of light

       ★

violets and forget-
      me-nots
heat pimples

on spring's face
      spring the year's
trough

      mushroom-free
disgrace
      interregnum season
not sweltering
      nor frost-encased

unless
      following further
into the woods

      this girl
scanner of bark roots
      and stumps

turn up
      following where
woodland-

      haunting
big cat Hamish
      slinks

      woodears
scarlet elfcups
      velvet shanks

     *

voiding a potty
      down the
garden drain
      where a capsized water-

boatman's drowned
      by the Bridget-
in-her-Bravery
      and spreading

elderflower
      find a three-
legged cat
      exultant over

biscuits left
      on the window-
ledge reached
      by his sinew-

sidle squirrel
        stomp with
at its fulcrum
        a furred back

        arched over—
miàù—
        his stitched-
up stump

     *

wood anemone
        of the musky
        leaves

you'll hear called
        windflowers
        and yet whose

seeds in a century
        venture
        not far

the width of my
        outstretched
        arms

reluctant traveler
        by whom we know
        the woods' age

a millennium pass-
        ing where
        over the burn

we cross
        the small
        low bridge

        *

behind
        its membrane
inside the jelly
        in the quarry
pond hides
        preserved
the almost-
        tadpole's eye
inside
        the May snow
and frost
        come on
without warning
        canceling
this year's
        tadpole/
frog supply

        *

from sofa to high
        in a yew
surprised
        in the woods
the cat is the link
        from within

to without
        sticky
willies seeding

                    the rug
        then rolling in clart
                    in the basin

        and off to follow
                    badger and
        pine marten

                    trails
        gone for days
                    out far

                    *

        Elizabeth Blackwell
                    Aberdeen-born
        yoked to a rogue
                    husband-cousin
        lives on the fly
                    driven by debt
        sketches engraves
                    the medicinal plants
        of A Curious Herbal
                    variously useful
        for combating
                    convulsions
        apoplexy
                    palsy fits
        and vertigo
                    pre-Linnaeus so
        no agreed names
                    her husband
        in prison supplies
                    the Latin
        loses his head
                    on a Swedish
        chopping block

        Blackwell
transplants to Chelsea
            where the thread
of her life
            is lost in tangles
like corn-
            poppy roots
whose flowers
            "are cooling,
incline to sleep"
            or rather
innocent stupor
            in which we await
those other
            slumbers
the grave
            keeps

            *

self-heal
            favored among
cemetery flowers

            fringing
this suicide's grave
            this peeled

illegible stone
            petals in oblong
clusters

            on the flat
graves' flooring

                its tidy
seedheads
                that remain

even after flowering

                *

deadly nightshade
                belladonna
atropa sprouting
                at the edge

of the park
                bell-shaped flower
biding its hour
                for the blue-into-black

                of the berries'
dark promise
                of creeping
paralysis

                and whose juice
squeezed onto
                the pupils

like chaser
                on shot
will cause
                them fash-

ionably—batting

their lashes
      at death—
to dilate

        *

night sky old
      zinc bucket
with clattering

        round it
stars
        Cancer's
claws scraping

the rim
      while over
the top of the hill

      cavort
in a phosphorus
      flash

the merry dancers

        *

white flowers
      spiraling down
its stem creeping

      lady's-tresses
orchid the size
      of my thumb

from which I know
        these woods a patch
of ancient forest

        islands of old
Caledonia
        reaching out to touch

across the interruptions
        of business park
garden center

        Barratt home hutch
where I sit
        and read of flowers

like this orchid
        beyond the culvert
pipe and ditch

        *

"gather ye fungi
        while ye may"

said Herrick never
        mushrooms
mere "excrement

        of the earth"
to his age

        witches' playthings
to the Romantics
        too

                    lower than
"the meanest flower"
                    passed over

unseen
            but planting
the clammy kiss

            of their names
tawny grisettes
            blushers

panthercaps
            on your tongue
here now

            ⋆

            even among dark
asphodel meadows of his
            underworld ramble
Odysseus encounters
not a single corpse-fed 'shroom

            ⋆

vomit forth the baneful pest (Theophrastus)

            ⋆

            meadow-grown
mushrooms are best
            distrust all others (Horace)

*

        nor will a youth be
esteemed higher than she who
        seeing her feckless
spendthrift parents acquires the
art of foraging mushrooms (Juvenal)

*

        Had Nature an Apostate
        That Mushroom—it is Him! (Dickinson)

        a girl's not
a flower but may
        be a mushroom

thriving in shadows
        of her own
choosing

        slippery furtive

transient
        though no more

than I
        growing
where I decline

        manifesting
to such as know
        where to look

but should
        the blundering
predator

               swoop
retracting
            soon enough

sly sickener
            all they would take

            *

for my mother at seventy-five

from July's shimmer
               up the long lane I'd
save for you shaken
               from their yellowy

anthers and coating
               the child's fingers
dog rose seeds
               dust of a young year

before the petals
               fading fuse
to rose-hips

               in heavy autumn
but for now shadows
               on summer's skin
among the nettles
               needing only

their rough acre
               on the reservoir's
edge where I see you
               keep watch

by the breeze-
                veined waters full of
their fluid occasions
                a tap turning

the tide of dailiness
                sieved through years
until the watcher
                you becomes me

and that life
                this one or wherever
along that stream
                we are now

                ★

would it could
                stay the gorse
                bells' yellow

framing
                the lochan basin
                unhooking now

for the year
                and back
                bristling

into the pages
                of Mary
                McMurtie's Scottish

Wild Flowers
                for the duration
                packed away

*

our daughter seeing
        chanterelles grow
on a dead mouse
        under a leaf

rolls in the leaves
        announces
"we can be
        mushrooms too"

        *

"again again"
        child's foot
among roots
        releasing

a spore-cloud
        to trail
next year's puff-
        balls over

the village
        and beyond
a body all lung
        deflating

and re-inflating
        the wind self-
pursuing run
        to ground   sown

*

yes yes to
      the rusty loch go
there to twist wolfsbane
      for poison wine

that purple and more
      autumn-tinged
purple spread
      and glow

as the columns of rose
      willowherb begin
to slow

      and blasted now
row upon row

      of wool-white
beards are all
      they have to show

*

beyond the village
      all day long
from a castle estate

      the clearances bought
      the echo
of shotguns clearing

      their throats
tartan of feathers
      and guts

you see where
       the odd escapee

makes it not
       for long
to the roads

      *

inland and upwards
       finally along the line
of incision exposure

       makes in a hiddenness
frost under the nails
       and the valley fingers

pulling on
       autumn's gloves again
in all this morning

       smirr where I ask
a dog-walker on the basin
       under the hill-fort

where to find
       the volcanic springs risen
and petrified under

       a meter of overburden
sedimentary textures
       preserving the free-

sporing rhynia
       in life position where
the colonizers grew

                    to climax communities
technical term
                    the nitrogen hoarders

in their carpet of roots
                    with branching present
the highland boundary fault

                    runs under the Romanesque
church past the burn
                    I tell myself crossing

out of our secular
                    weather into that further
past and soft tissue

                    there is soft tissue
present in the chert
                    these fossils not

aquatic flowers but agents
                    of terrestrialization
earliest known

                    relationship between
plant and animal
                    out of the water

and parasites too
                    the nematodes in
the translucent matrix

                    eating their host out
from the inside
                    prehistory stepping

gamely forth from
         the stony seabed
every worm's stomach
         chamber its own
self-seeding grave
                  outpacing

the Devonian
         but how far along
the now have we come

         I wonder to where
I am standing

         here breathing
through the world's
         oldest known lungs

         *

death in infancy
         the most banal
thing in the
         world to judge
from these Victorian
         inscriptions
son of daughter
         of the above
our own sweet children
         at play among
the tombs in their
         clean Presbyterian
grace with here
         and there

a Christmas Tennents
       can unopened
on the green
       glass chippings
opaque sorrows
       of a Latvian child
teenaged girl
       fixed in her
Snapchat filter
       a selvedge of new
graves along the
       overflow plot
awkward arrivals
       at a village-hall
disco awaiting
       the safety of
numbers among
       whom in time
lay me too in this
       civic sub-wilderness
mown once a week
       spring and summer
because where else
       I suppose if
not among
       the plastic flowers
seedless
       and undying

     *

I salute that various field (James Schuyler)

and this was the land
       of plenty

a plucked primrose
        tight in her hand

where sulfur tufts
        that bitter toxin

march from a pine
        stump over

a carpet of
        unseen roots

and *'s i b' fhasa*
        dhomh mholadh

she it was easy to praise
        child I will

scoop and carry
        over that patch-

work where the hill
        starts to rise

ACKNOWLEDGMENTS

Grateful acknowledgment is made to the Arts Council of Ireland/ An Chomhairle Ealaíon for the award of a literature bursary.

Thanks to the editors of the following publications in which versions of these poems previously appeared: *Anthropocene, Poetry Birmingham Literary Journal, Bad Lilies, Echtrai, The Irish Times, Gitanjali and Beyond, Times Literary Supplement, Axon, New York Review of Books, London Review of Books, The Stinging Fly, Blackbox Manifold, PN Review, Our Lady of the Snows* (Clutag Press), *The Fourth Craw* (Glyph Press), *Companions of His Thoughts More Green: Quatercentenary Poems for Andrew Marvell* (Broken Sleep Press), *Walter de la Mare: A Critical Appraisal* (Liverpool University Press), *Reading the Future: New Writing for Ireland Celebrating 250 Years of Hodges Figgis* (Arlen House), *Four Rivers Deep: A deep map of Scotland's Don and Dee and Western Australia's Swan and Canning Rivers* (UWA Publishing).

Le taing do Niall Ó Gallchóir agus Pàdraig MacAoidh.